1904

SAMANTHA'S COOK BOOK

*A Peek at
Dining in the
Past with Meals
You Can Cook Today*

PLEASANT COMPANY PUBLICATIONS

Published by Pleasant Company Publications
For information, address: Book Editor, Pleasant Company Publications,
8400 Fairway Place, P.O. Box 620998, Middleton, WI 53562.

First Edition.
Printed in the United States of America.
95 96 97 98 99 WCR 10 9 8 7 6

The American Girls Collection® is a
registered trademark of Pleasant Company.

PICTURE CREDITS
The following individuals and organizations have generously
given permission to reprint illustrations in this book:
Pages 2, 3, 5—State Historical Society of Wisconsin; 7—Strong Museum;
8—State Historical Society of Wisconsin; 9—GRAPE NUTS is a registered
trademark of Kraft General Foods, Inc.; 11—State Historical Society of Wisconsin;
13—Taken from *Chronicles of Saratoga* by Evelyn Barrett Britten © 1959 with
permission from *The Saratogian*; 16—Museum of the City of New York, The Byron
Collection; 18—Strong Museum; 19—Nabisco Foods Group; 21—Joseph J. Pennell
Collection, Kansas Collection, University of Kansas Libraries; 25—Strong Museum;
29—The Bettmann Archive (bottom); 30—Strong Museum; 31—State Historical
Society of Wisconsin; 33—From the Collections of Henry Ford Museum & Greenfield
Village; 36—Taken from *American Home Life 1880-1930* with permission from Grand
Met Pillsbury Company; 37—1904-1906 H. Winslow Fegley photograph from the
Schwenkfelder Library in Pennsburg, Pennsylvania; 41—State Historical Society
of Wisconsin (top); 42—Library of Congress, Washington, D.C./Courtesy
Mrs. Sharp's Traditions Collections of Antique Images;
43—Strong Museum; 44—Newport Historical Society.

Edited by Jodi Evert and Jeanne Thieme
Written by Polly Athan, Terri Braun, Jodi Evert, and Jeanne Thieme
Designed and Art Directed by Jane S. Varda
Produced by Karen Bennett, Laura Paulini, and Pat Tuchscherer
Cover Illustration by Luann Roberts
Inside Illustrations by Susan Mahal
Photography by Mark Salisbury
Historical and Picture Research by Polly Athan, Rebecca Sample Bernstein,
Terri Braun, Jodi Evert, Robyn Hansen, and Doreen Smith
Recipe Testing Coordinated by Jean doPico
Food Styling by Janice Bell
Prop Research by Leslie Cakora

Library of Congress Cataloging-in-Publication Data

Samantha's cookbook : a peek at dining in the past with meals you can cook today /
[edited by Jodi Evert ; written by Polly Athan . . . et al. ; inside illustration
by Susan Mahal ; photography by Mark Salisbury]. — 1st ed.
p. cm.
ISBN 1-56247-114-7 (softcover)
1. Cookery—Juvenile literature. 2. Cookery, American—Juvenile literature. 3. United
States—Social life and customs—20th century—Juvenile literature. [1. Cookery,
American. 2. United States—Social life and customs—20th century.]
I. Evert, Jodi.
II. Athan, Polly. III. Mahal, Susan, ill. IV. Salisbury, Mark, ill.
TX652.5.S26 1994 641.5973'0901—dc20 94-12059 CIP AC

CONTENTS

S pecial thanks to all the children and adults who tested the recipes and gave us their valuable comments:

Emily Ballweg and her mother Amy Ballweg
Amelia Barber and her mother M. Gale Barber
Meredith Barbera and her mother Cindy Barbera
Julia Barton and her mother Wendy Barton
Michelle Bridge and her mother Becky Bridge
Alisa Brown and her mother Marlene Brown
Katie Bush and her mother Kathryn Bush
Ashleigh Conrad and her mother Glenda Conrad
Cassie Dabel and her mother Ginny Dabel
Emily Dresen and her mother Mary Jo Dresen
Hannah Flake and her mother Kathy Flake
Carla Gilbertson and her mother Lois Gilbertson
Emily Giovanni and her mother Deanna Giovanni
Allison Guilfoil and her mother Connie Guilfoil
Lauren Hackbarth and her mother Kim Hackbarth
Elizabeth Heymann and her mother Jane Heymann
Shannon Johnson and her mother Julie Johnson
Amanda Keller and her mother Sharon Keller
Meagan Lowenberg and her mother Cheryl Lowenberg
Marianna March and her mother Donna March
Mallory Mason and her mother Janet Mason
Meredith Newlin and her mother Karen Watson-Newlin
Saree Olkes and her mother Judy Olkes
Elizabeth Solberg and her mother Peggy Solberg
Vanessa Theis and her mother LaVonne Theis
Rebecca Theisen and her mother Deanna Theisen
Heather Thue and her mother Jane Thue
Nick Young and his mother Lois Young

DINING IN THE EARLY 1900s

In the early 1900s, when Samantha was growing up, kitchen equipment made cooking faster and easier than it had been before. Samantha's house had a kitchen sink with running water, a new gas stove, and an early kind of refrigerator called an *icebox*. But Samantha didn't use them often. In 1904, servants cooked for wealthy American families. Some people thought a proper young lady's place was in the dining room, where she learned to be the perfect hostess at formal meals.

An icebox.

When Samantha was a girl, lots of food was served at every meal. But the most lavish meals were planned when company came to dinner. When a wealthy lady like Grandmary invited guests, she planned the dinner party days in advance. A servant delivered invitations. The cook ordered special foods from the grocer and butcher.

Cookbooks had a place in the kitchen and the parlor because elegant hostesses and their cooks were interested in all the latest recipes. Some cookbooks also gave advice about proper behavior, or *etiquette*, in the dining room.

Learning about cooking and dining in the early 1900s will help you understand what it was like to grow up the way Samantha did. Cooking the foods she ate will help bring history alive for you and your family.

SAMANTHA ❧ 1904

Samantha Parkington was an orphan, raised by her grandmother in the early 1900s. Wealthy Americans like Grandmary followed strict rules of behavior in the dining room.

SERVANTS AND SERVING

SILENT SERVANTS

Servants did not speak to the guests or to one another in the dining room. The hostess did not usually speak to the servants, either. The butler made sure the meal went smoothly.

Grandmary was the head of Samantha's household. She planned the menus for every meal. When she invited guests for special meals, she even decided where they would sit. But her elegant life would have been almost impossible without servants.

Mrs. Hawkins, the cook, prepared all the food. She ordered the groceries after the menus were planned. She knew where to get the freshest fruits and vegetables, as well as the best cuts of meat and fish. Mrs. Hawkins got help in the kitchen from a scullery maid who did the dishes and helped keep the kitchen clean.

Mr. Hawkins, the butler, was one of the most respected servants in Grandmary's house. His biggest job was serving all the meals. He also made sure that meals began on time. Butlers were in charge of all the servants who worked in the dining room. Usually one or more maids helped him serve meals at the table. The maids also worked in the *butler's pantry*, a small room between the kitchen and dining room. Between meals, they polished all the silver and made sure the lamps and candles were in perfect condition. And they kept the pantry spotlessly clean.

Grandmary made sure the servants did their jobs correctly. Many servants, like Mr. and Mrs. Hawkins, lived in the house where they worked. At night, a butler like Mr. Hawkins locked the front door after everyone else had gone to bed.

SETTING SAMANTHA'S TABLE

In 1904, etiquette books told hostesses how to set a proper table for elegant dining. Mr. Hawkins instructed and supervised the maids to be sure everything was perfect.

The servants covered the table with a felt *silence cloth* to soften the rattle of knives, forks, and dishes. Then a tablecloth was laid over the silence cloth. The center crease of the tablecloth divided the table exactly in half. Next the servants placed a small white lace or embroidered cloth, called a *centerpiece*, in the middle of the table. On it, they placed a flower arrangement or fruit bowl.

For dinner parties, servants would place a candlestick at each of the four corners of the centerpiece. Fancy dishes of appetizers and salted nuts sat between the candlesticks.

Each person's plate, glass, and silverware was called a *cover*. Etiquette books gave exact directions for where to put each dish and piece of silver. For example, the books said that the foot of the water goblet should just touch the tip of the blade of the longest knife being used for that meal. Each diner might have a small dish of salt, called a *salt cellar*, with a tiny spoon. A large cloth napkin was placed to the left of each plate. For dinner parties, a dinner roll was folded into each napkin. Name cards told the guests where to sit.

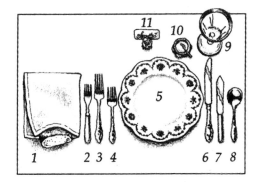

A COVER

Each person's table setting was called a cover. A cover for a formal dinner might include:

1. napkin	7. fish knife
2. fish fork	8. soup spoon
3. roast fork	9. water goblet
4. salad fork	10. salt cellar
5. plate	11. name card
6. roast knife	

These students are learning how to set a proper table.

TIPS FOR TODAY'S COOKS

MEASURING FLOUR

A good cook measures exactly. Here is a hint for measuring flour. Spoon the flour into a measuring cup, heaping it up over the top. Then use the spoon handle to level off the flour. Don't shake or tap the cup.

TABLE OF MEASUREMENTS

3 teaspoons = 1 tablespoon
2 cups = 1 pint
2 pints = 1 quart
4 cups = 1 quart

Y ou'll find below a list of things that every good cook should know. But this is the most important tip: **work with an adult.** This is the safe way for you to work in the kitchen. Cooking together is fun, too. It's a tradition American families have always shared. Keep it alive today!

1. Choose a time that suits you and the adult who's cooking with you, so that you will both enjoy working together in the kitchen.

2. Wash your hands with soap before you handle food. Wear an apron, tie back your hair, and roll up your sleeves.

3. Read a recipe carefully, all the way through, before you start it. Look at the pictures. They will help you understand the steps.

4. Gather all the ingredients and equipment you will need before you start to cook. Put everything where you can reach it easily.

5. Ask an adult to show you how to peel, cut, or grate with sharp kitchen tools. Always use a chopping board to save kitchen counters.

6. Pay attention while using knives so that you don't cut your fingers! Remember, a good, sharp knife is safer than a dull one.

7. When you stir or mix, hold the bowl or pan steady on a flat surface, not in your arms.

8. Make sure your mixing bowls, pots, and pans are the right size. If they are too small, you'll probably spill. If pots and pans are too large, foods will burn more easily.

9. Clean up spills right away.

10. Pots and pans will be less likely to spill on the stove if you turn the handles toward the side.

11. Have an adult handle hot pans. Don't use the stove burners or the oven without permission or supervision.

12. Turn off the burner or the oven as soon as a dish is cooked.

13. Potholders and oven mitts will protect you from burns. Use them when you touch anything hot. Protect kitchen counters by putting trivets or cooling racks under hot pots and pans.

14. Keep hot foods hot and cold foods cold. If you plan to make things early and serve them later, store them properly. Foods that could spoil belong in the refrigerator. Wrap foods well.

15. If you decide to make a whole meal, be sure to plan so that all the food will be ready when you are ready to serve it.

16. Cleanup is part of cooking, too. Leave the kitchen at least as clean as you found it. Wash all the dishes, pots, and pans. Sweep the floor. Throw away the garbage.

COOKING IN THE EARLY 1900s

In Samantha's time, cooking was considered a science as well as an art. In cooking schools, young women learned about the "basic food factors"—proteins, carbohydrates, fats, minerals, and water. People didn't know about vitamins in 1904!

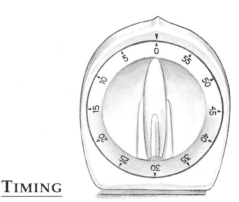

TIMING

When a recipe gives two cooking times—for example, when it says, "bake 25 to 30 minutes"—first set the timer for the shorter time. If the food is not done when the timer rings, give it more time.

BREAKFAST

An ice delivery wagon.

When Mrs. Hawkins, the cook, got up to prepare breakfast, Samantha was still fast asleep. Mrs. Hawkins turned on the gas oven to warm it for baking. When the milkman arrived, he delivered milk, cream, and butter for the day. He also took empty milk bottles from the day before. The next deliveryman brought blocks of fresh ice for the *icebox*, a wooden chest with room for food and a big block of ice. The icebox kept foods fresh and chilled. But the ice usually melted by the end of the day.

A maid woke Grandmary and Samantha. She opened Samantha's curtains and laid out clothes for Samantha to wear. Samantha dressed in a hurry. She smelled something wonderful. Then she remembered that blueberry muffins were on the breakfast menu. Breakfast was usually the lightest meal of the day. But in wealthy households like Samantha's, this "light" meal usually included fruit, meat or fish, eggs, potatoes, and toast, muffins, bread, or biscuits! Most adults drank tea or coffee, but children often drank hot cocoa.

An ad for cocoa from Samantha's time.

BREAKFAST

ঔ

Strawberries with Cream

•

Ham Slice

•

Cheese Omelet

•

Saratoga Potatoes

•

Blueberry Muffins

By eight o'clock, Samantha and Grandmary were seated at the breakfast table. Mr. Hawkins and the maids brought the dishes to the dining room. Samantha unfolded her napkin and placed it across her knees. Then she sat quietly and waited to be served.

While she ate, Samantha tried hard to take small bites and chew them quietly. When she ate her muffin, she broke it into pieces first instead of biting into it. Grandmary nodded to Samantha to let her know that she was pleased with Samantha's behavior in the dining room.

STRAWBERRIES WITH CREAM

Juicy strawberries float in a bowl of thick white cream.

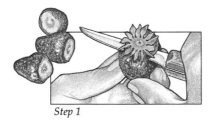

Step 1

INGREDIENTS

3 cups fresh strawberries
1 pint heavy cream
½ cup sugar

EQUIPMENT

Paring knife
Colander
Cutting board
Serving bowl
Cream pitcher
Small sugar bowl

DIRECTIONS   *6 servings*

1. Use the paring knife to remove the stem and leaves from each strawberry.

2. Put the strawberries into the colander and rinse them well under cold water.

3. Cut any large strawberries into bite-size pieces. Put the strawberries into the serving bowl.

4. Pour cream into the cream pitcher. Put sugar in the sugar bowl. That way your guests can put the amount of cream and sugar they prefer on their strawberries. ≈

SUMMER STRAWBERRIES

In 1904, girls like Samantha enjoyed picking strawberries for fun. Some people made the berries into fancy desserts, but others simply enjoyed eating them in the shade on a warm summer afternoon. They held the washed berries by the stem, dipped them in sugar, and ate them with their fingers!

HAM SLICE

INGREDIENTS

2-pound fully cooked
 ham slice
2 tablespoons water

EQUIPMENT

Cutting board
Knife
Measuring spoon
Skillet
Fork
Serving plate

*A thick, juicy ham slice was perfect
for a proper breakfast in 1904.*

DIRECTIONS *6 servings*

1. Place the ham slice on the cutting board. Have
   an adult help you trim away the fat from the
   outside edges. Cut the ham slice into serving-
   size pieces.

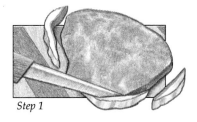

Step 1

2. Measure the water into the skillet. Turn the
   heat to medium high. Let the water get warm.

3. Put the ham pieces into the skillet and cook
   them about 3 minutes.

4. Turn over the pieces with a fork. Cook them for
   3 more minutes. Then put the ham pieces onto
   a serving plate. ❧

Every golden granule of
Grape=Nuts
contains the sturdy nourishment of wheat
and barley — nothing left out that could
build strength and health.
"There's a Reason"

A HEALTHIER START

*Cereal makers urged families to eat less
meat and more cereals, like Shredded
Wheat® or Grape Nuts®, for breakfast.
But not everyone liked these new health
foods. They called them "shredded
doormats," "gripe nuts," or
"eata-heapa-hay"!*

CHEESE OMELET

This omelet has a creamy cheese filling melted in the center.

INGREDIENTS

6 eggs
1/2 teaspoon salt
1/8 teaspoon pepper
4 tablespoons water
2 tablespoons butter
1/2 cup grated cheese

EQUIPMENT

Mixing bowl
Fork
Measuring cup
   and spoons
Large skillet
Spatula
Serving dish

DIRECTIONS   *6 servings*

1. Crack the eggs into the mixing bowl.

2. Use the fork to beat the eggs until they are well mixed.

3. Add the salt, pepper, and water.

4. Continue beating the mixture with the fork until it is foamy.

5. Melt the butter in the skillet over medium-high heat until it is bubbly. Be careful not to let the butter burn.

6. Pour the egg mixture into the skillet.

7. As the eggs cook, use the spatula to push them gently toward the middle of the skillet. Have an adult help you tilt the pan slightly so the uncooked eggs move to the outside.

Step 1

Step 7

8. When the bottom of the omelet is lightly browned and the eggs are firm, sprinkle the grated cheese over half of the omelet.

9. Have an adult help you lift and fold the other half of the omelet over the cheese.

Steps 8, 9

10. Lower the heat to medium low and allow the omelet to cook until the cheese is fully melted, about 2 to 3 minutes.

11. Have an adult help you slide the omelet out of the pan and onto the serving dish. Serve the omelet while it is hot. ❧

EGG COLLECTION

In 1904, farm children collected eggs each morning. Families kept some of their eggs and sold the rest to an egg dealer, who visited their farms once or twice a week. Then the dealer shipped the eggs by train into cities, where some of the eggs ended up on breakfast tables like Samantha's!

SARATOGA POTATOES

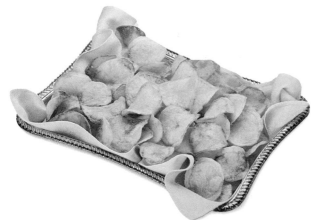

Fried Saratoga potatoes add a crispy crunch to breakfast.

INGREDIENTS

4 large potatoes
Cold water
8 ice cubes
2 cups shortening
Salt

EQUIPMENT

Vegetable peeler
Large bowl
Grater
Paper towels
Rubber spatula
Measuring cup
Large skillet
Slotted spoon or skimmer
Aluminum pie pan
Serving plate

DIRECTIONS   *6 servings*

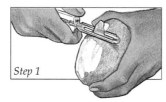

Step 1

1. Have an adult help you peel the potatoes.

2. Put cold water into the bowl until it is half full. Then add the ice cubes.

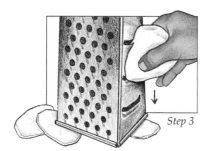

Step 3

3. Have an adult help you rub the potatoes over the wide slicer on the grater to cut them into very thin, round slices.

4. As the potatoes are sliced, put them into the bowl of ice water to remove some of the starch.

5. Drain a handful of potato slices on the paper towels. Pat the tops with more paper towels. Drying the potatoes keeps the shortening from splattering when you put them into the skillet.

6. Use the rubber spatula to add the shortening to the skillet. Melt the shortening over medium-high heat until it is very hot.

7. Have an adult help you use the slotted spoon or skimmer to put 1 potato slice into the shortening to test it. The shortening should bubble around the potato. If the potato turns brown quickly, the shortening is too hot—turn down the heat a little.

Step 7

8. Carefully move the rest of the dried slices from the paper towels into the hot shortening.

9. As the potatoes cook, separate any slices that stick together.

10. Fry the potatoes for 4 to 5 minutes, or until they turn a light golden color. Then have an adult help you remove them from the skillet.

11. Put the hot slices into the pie pan and shake salt lightly over them. Then slide them onto the serving plate.

12. Fry the rest of the potatoes in the same way. If the shortening becomes too hot or smoky, turn down the heat. 🥢

SARATOGA POTATOES

This picture shows Moon's Lake House, a fashionable resort located in Saratoga Springs, New York. In 1853, an American Indian named Pete Francis invented Saratoga potatoes at this resort after a diner complained that the fried potatoes were too thick.

BLUEBERRY MUFFINS

*Fresh-baked blueberry muffins
will delight your guests.*

INGREDIENTS

Shortening to grease
  muffin pan
1 cup fresh blueberries
3 tablespoons shortening
3 tablespoons sugar
1 egg
1 cup milk
1¾ cups flour
3 teaspoons baking powder
¾ teaspoon salt
Butter and jam

EQUIPMENT

Muffin pan
Paper towels
Strainer
Measuring cups
  and spoons
Large mixing bowl
Wooden spoon
Sifter
Potholders
Toothpick
Basket or plate

DIRECTIONS   *12 muffins*

1. Preheat the oven to 400°. Use shortening to lightly grease each muffin cup.

2. Put the blueberries into the strainer, and then rinse them under cold running water. Drain them on paper towels.

3. Measure 3 tablespoons of shortening into the mixing bowl. Slowly stir the sugar into the shortening until the mixture is light and fluffy.

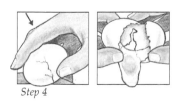

Step 4

4. Crack the egg into the bowl. Beat the mixture well.

5. Stir in the milk. Mix well.

6. Hold the sifter over the mixing bowl. Measure the flour, baking powder, and salt into the sifter. Sift them into the mixing bowl.

7. Stir gently, just enough to moisten the flour mixture.

8. Carefully stir the blueberries into the mixture.

9. Fill each muffin cup ⅔ full.

Step 9

10. Bake the muffins on the middle oven rack for 20 to 25 minutes.

11. Insert a toothpick into 1 of the muffins. If it comes out clean, the muffins are done.

12. Have an adult remove the muffin pan from the oven. Let the muffins cool for a few minutes. Then arrange them in a basket or on a plate and serve them with butter and jam. 🐚

GAS STOVES

"Modern" kitchens in the early 1900s had gas stoves. Temperatures were easier to control with a gas stove than with a wood-burning cookstove. And the cook did not have to constantly feed wood to the fire.

DINNER

An elegant dining room like Samantha's.

Samantha loved the gleam of silver and the glitter of crystal in Grandmary's candlelit dining room. Dinner was a formal occasion in wealthy homes in 1904. Girls like Samantha dressed up for dinner every evening and practiced their best manners. Sometimes they even wore gloves in the dining room!

At formal dinner parties, gentlemen escorted ladies to the table when the butler announced, "Dinner is served." Everyone sat at an assigned place, marked with a name card. Often there was a small menu card that listed what would be served—everything "from soup to nuts."

Dinner was served in courses. Each course included several dishes of food. Some very fancy dinners had as many as 18 courses. Samantha's dinner for guests had five courses, served in the English style.

At an English-style dinner, the hostess "helped" the servants with their work. Grandmary ladled soup onto soup plates or tossed the salad. Then servants brought the food to each guest. Guests "helped" the servants, too. They passed the appetizers around the table when Grandmary suggested they might. A gentleman like Uncle Gard or Admiral Beemis "served" the main course by carving the roast.

A family eating dinner in the early 1900s.

Grandmary also served dessert with the help of her guests, who passed the plates around the table after she filled them. And the hostess always poured coffee at the end of the meal.

Since the hostess had "served" the food, it was polite for guests to have second helpings and to talk about how good everything tasted. At more formal meals, talking about the food was very rude!

DINNER

First Course

Cream of Carrot Soup

Celery, Radishes, Olives

•

Second Course

Roasted Beef Tenderloin

Mashed Potatoes

Fresh Green Beans

Corn Oysters

•

Third Course

French Salad

Cheeses

•

Fourth Course

Ice Cream Snowballs

Dainties

•

Fifth Course

Fresh Fruit

•

Coffee, Nuts, Raisins

CREAM OF CARROT SOUP

Garnish this creamy orange-colored soup with thin carrot curls.

INGREDIENTS

1 pound carrots
2 cups chicken broth
2 tablespoons butter
2 tablespoons flour
$\frac{1}{2}$ teaspoon salt
$\frac{1}{8}$ teaspoon cayenne
   pepper
1 cup half-and-half
Crackers

EQUIPMENT

Vegetable peeler
Knife
Cutting board
2-quart saucepan with lid
Measuring cups
   and spoons
Fork
Colander
Large bowl
Potato masher
3-quart saucepan
Wooden spoon
Ladle
Soup bowls

DIRECTIONS   *6 servings*

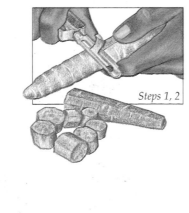
Steps 1, 2

1. Have an adult help you peel the carrots. Rinse the peeled carrots under cold water.

2. Cut the carrots into $\frac{1}{2}$-inch slices.

3. Put the sliced carrots into the 2-quart saucepan. Add the chicken broth.

4. Cook the carrots and broth over medium-high heat. When the broth begins to *boil*, or bubble rapidly, turn the heat down to medium low.

5. Cover the saucepan. Cook the carrots for 20 minutes or until they are very soft and break apart when pierced with the fork.

COLORFUL CARROTS

Some people thought carrots did not belong on a proper dining table because their color was too bright!

6. Place the colander in the large bowl. Have an adult pour the broth and carrots through the colander, catching the carrots in the colander. Save the broth to use in Step 11.

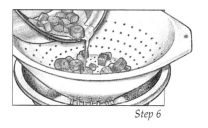

Step 6

7. Put the drained carrots back into the 2-quart saucepan. Mash them until they are very smooth. Set the pan aside.

Step 7

8. In the 3-quart saucepan, melt the butter over medium heat. Then stir in the flour.

9. Cook the butter and flour for 1 minute over low heat, stirring constantly.

10. Add the mashed carrots, salt, and cayenne pepper. Stir to mix them together.

11. Slowly stir in the broth. Turn the heat up to medium high and cook for 10 minutes. Stir often.

12. Add the half-and-half. Heat the soup slowly, stirring constantly. Do not let the soup boil.

13. Ladle the hot soup into bowls. Serve with crackers. ❧

DON'T UNEEDA BISCUIT?

Until 1898, crackers were sold in barrels. Then the National Biscuit Company packaged them in boxes and called them Uneeda Biscuits. The slicker boy in the advertisements became so popular that children often dressed like him for parties and parades.

ROASTED BEEF TENDERLOIN

When beef tenderloin is cooked to perfection, the center is still pink.

INGREDIENTS

1 teaspoon salt
½ teaspoon pepper
2-pound trimmed beef
   tenderloin, tied for
   baking
Fresh parsley
1 lemon

EQUIPMENT

Measuring spoons
Sturdy baking pan with
   1-inch sides
Potholders
Tinfoil
Paper towels
Serving platter
Paring knife
Cutting board
Kitchen shears
2 forks
Carving knife
Dinner plates

DIRECTIONS   *6 servings*

1. Preheat the oven to 450°.

2. Sprinkle the salt and pepper evenly over the meat on all sides. Then put the meat into the pan.

3. Have an adult put the pan on the middle oven rack. Bake 30 minutes for medium-rare meat, 35 minutes for medium.

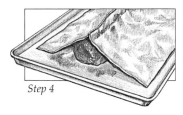

Step 4

4. Have an adult remove the pan from the oven and cover the meat with foil. Let it "rest" for 15 minutes. The meat keeps on cooking as it rests. It is easier to cut after it rests.

5. While the meat rests, wash the fresh parsley under cold water. Dry it with paper towels.

6. Pull sprigs of parsley off the stems. Place them onto the serving platter to make a "bed" for the meat.

7. Have an adult help you cut the lemon into slices. Arrange them on the platter.

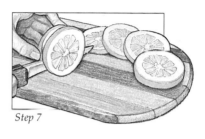
Step 7

8. Just before serving, uncover the meat. Use kitchen shears to cut the string.

9. Use the 2 forks to lift the meat onto the serving platter.

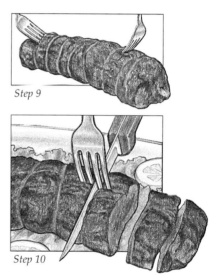
Step 9

10. Use 1 fork to hold the roasted meat steady. Have an adult help you cut the meat into slices that are 1 inch thick. Use a sawing motion.

11. Lift 1 slice of meat onto each dinner plate. 🐚

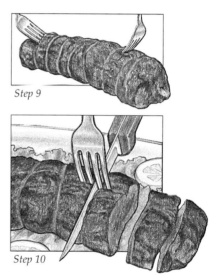
Step 10

BUTCHER SHOPS

There were no electric freezers in 1904. Cooks had to make frequent trips to the butcher shop to buy fresh meat. Or, if a cook's employer had a telephone, she could call in an order and have it delivered to her doorstep!

MASHED POTATOES

Melt butter into these creamy mashed potatoes.

INGREDIENTS

6 medium potatoes
Water
1 teaspoon salt
$\frac{1}{2}$ cup milk
4 tablespoons butter
$\frac{1}{4}$ teaspoon salt

EQUIPMENT

Vegetable peeler
Knife and cutting board
3-quart saucepan with lid
Measuring cup
    and spoons
Fork
Potato masher
Spoon
Serving bowl

DIRECTIONS   *6 servings*

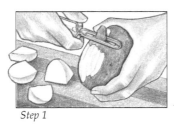

Step 1

1. Have an adult help you peel the potatoes. Cut each potato into 4 pieces.

2. Put the potatoes into the saucepan and cover them with water. Add 1 teaspoon salt.

3. Cover the pan and place it over high heat. When the water begins to *boil*, or bubble quickly, turn the heat down to medium.

4. Let the potatoes boil for 20 minutes, or until they are soft when pierced with a fork.

5. Have an adult drain the hot water from the pan of cooked potatoes.

Step 6

6. Mash the potatoes in the pan. Add the milk, butter, and $\frac{1}{4}$ teaspoon salt. Keep mashing until the potatoes are light and fluffy. Spoon them into the serving bowl. 🍂

FRESH GREEN BEANS

INGREDIENTS

1½ pounds fresh
  green beans
½ teaspoon salt
Cold water

EQUIPMENT

Colander
2-quart saucepan with lid
Measuring spoon
Serving bowl

*Add color and crunch to the meat
course with bright green beans.*

DIRECTIONS   *6 servings*

1. Put the green beans into the colander. Rinse them with cold running water. Then break off both ends of each bean. Throw the ends away.

2. Put the beans into the saucepan. Add the salt and just enough water to cover the beans.

3. Place the pan over high heat. When the water begins to *boil*, or bubble quickly, turn the heat down to medium low.

4. Cover the pan and let the beans *simmer*, or cook gently, for 10 minutes.

5. Have an adult help you pour the water and the beans into the colander at the sink. Put the beans into the serving bowl. 🐝

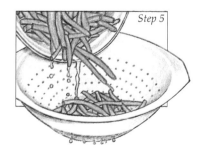

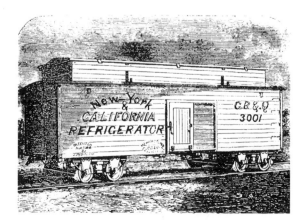

TRAVELING VEGETABLES

*By 1900, many fresh vegetables came to
American cities from California. They
traveled in refrigerated railroad cars.*

CORN OYSTERS

Corn patties shaped like oysters look elegant on the table.

INGREDIENTS

2 cups frozen corn kernels
¼ cup milk
⅓ cup flour
1 egg
½ teaspoon salt
¼ teaspoon pepper
2 tablespoons butter
2 tablespoons vegetable oil

EQUIPMENT

Colander
Medium mixing bowl
Measuring cups
 and spoons
Wooden spoon
Paper towels
Serving platter
10-inch skillet
Spoon
Spatula
Tinfoil

DIRECTIONS   *16 corn oysters*

1. Put the frozen corn into the colander. Rinse it with cold water until the ice crystals disappear.

2. Pour the corn into the bowl. Stir in the milk, flour, egg, salt, and pepper.

3. Lay paper towels on top of the platter. Then set it aside.

4. Place the skillet over medium-high heat. Add the butter and oil.

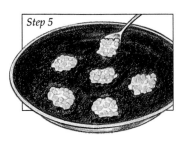

5. Use the wooden spoon to spread the melted butter and oil evenly in the skillet. Then have an adult help you put 6 small spoonfuls of the corn mixture into the skillet.

6. Let the corn oysters cook for 2 to 3 minutes, or until the bottoms are golden brown.

7. Use the spatula to turn the corn oysters gently.
Cook them for 2 or 3 minutes more, or until
both sides are golden brown.

8. Drain the corn oysters on the platter covered
with paper towels. Cover the platter with foil
to keep them warm.

9. Continue frying corn oysters in the same way
until the corn mixture is gone. You should have
about 16 corn oysters.

10. Remove the foil and paper towels from the
platter and serve the corn oysters hot. 🎗️

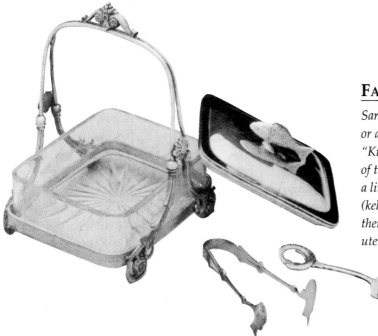

FASHIONABLE SEAFOOD

Sardines were popular **kickshaws**,
or appetizers, in Samantha's time.
"Kickshaws" was an English way
of trying to say the French words for
a little "something" — **quelque chose**
(kel-kah SHOWS). Sardines even had
their own special serving dishes and
utensils, as shown in this picture.

FRENCH SALAD

Fresh, crisp salads were a popular food in 1904.

INGREDIENTS

1 large head romaine
   lettuce
1 small bunch chives
1 teaspoon dried
   tarragon leaves
Salad dressing (*See page 27
to make your own.*)

EQUIPMENT

Colander
Paper towels
Clean, dry kitchen towel
Kitchen shears
Serving bowl
Measuring spoon
2 large spoons

DIRECTIONS   *6 servings*

1. Break off the lettuce leaves and put them into the colander. Don't use brown or wilted leaves.

2. Rinse the lettuce under very cold water. Then pat the lettuce leaves dry with the paper towels.

3. Tear the lettuce leaves into bite-size pieces and lay the pieces on the kitchen towel. Roll up the towel and put it in the refrigerator.

4. Snip the chives into tiny pieces with the kitchen shears. Put the snipped chives in the refrigerator.

5. Just before you are ready to serve the salad, put the lettuce into the serving bowl. Add the chives and sprinkle on the tarragon.

6. Toss the salad with dressing and serve.

Step 1

Step 3

DRESSING

INGREDIENTS

4 tablespoons tarragon
  vinegar
1 tablespoon water
1 teaspoon Dijon-style
  mustard
$\frac{1}{2}$ teaspoon salt
$\frac{1}{2}$ teaspoon sugar
$\frac{1}{4}$ teaspoon pepper
$\frac{1}{2}$ cup vegetable or
  olive oil

EQUIPMENT

1-pint jar with lid
Measuring cup
  and spoons

*Dressing was served from a fancy little pitcher called a **cruet**.*

DIRECTIONS   *6 servings*

1. Put the vinegar, water, mustard, salt, sugar, and pepper into the jar.

2. Screw the lid on the jar tightly. Shake it to blend the ingredients.

3. Add the oil. Put the lid back on the jar and shake it again, hard enough to mix the oil with all the other ingredients.

4. You can make the dressing early in the day and keep it in the jar. Shake it once more before tossing it with the salad. 🦢

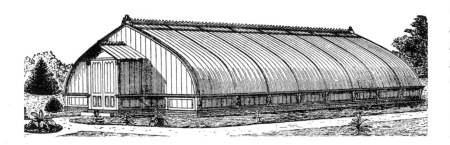

SEASONAL SALADS

*In the 1890s, only wealthy Americans ate green salads in the winter. Lettuce was grown near the city of Boston in heated glass buildings called **hothouses**. In 1903, sturdy iceberg lettuce was developed. Because it traveled well on refrigerated railroad cars, it could be shipped to more Americans than ever before.*

ICE CREAM SNOWBALLS

Roll vanilla ice cream in coconut to make this sweet summertime treat.

INGREDIENTS

1 quart vanilla ice cream
2 cups shredded coconut
12 ladyfinger cookies

EQUIPMENT

Measuring cup
Shallow bowl
Ice cream scoop
2 large spoons
Freezer container with lid

DIRECTIONS   *6 snowballs*

1. Put the ice cream into the refrigerator for 30 minutes or until it is soft enough to scoop.

2. Put the coconut into the bowl.

3. Scoop out a large ball of ice cream and drop it into the coconut.

Step 4

4. Use the 2 spoons to roll the ice cream around until it is covered with coconut.

5. Using a spoon, lift the ice cream snowball out of the bowl. Put it into the freezer container.

VANILLA

Vanilla was the most popular flavor of ice cream in Samantha's time, and it's still a favorite today. The vanilla plant originally came from Mexico and South America.

6. Repeat Steps 3, 4, and 5 until you have 6 ice cream snowballs. Keep the snowballs separated.

7. Cover the freezer container tightly so the coconut doesn't dry out. Freeze the ice cream snowballs several hours or overnight.

8. Take the container out of the freezer 15 minutes before you are ready to serve dessert. Serve each ice cream snowball with 2 cookies. ✤

THE FRUIT COURSE

Sometimes fresh fruit was used as a table decoration at elegant dinner parties. After the dessert course, a servant passed the fancy fruit bowl and guests helped themselves.

THE NATIONAL DESSERT

Ice cream was the national dessert in 1904, just as it is today. People of all ages flocked to ice cream parlors. Children often bought frozen dainties from **hokey-pokey men**, *or street vendors who sold inexpensive ice cream. In Samantha's time, a* **dainty** *was a small treat.*

FAVORITE FOODS

Girls learning to cook.

I n the early 1900s, many people believed that even wealthy girls should learn how to cook, as well as how to become proper hostesses. A poem written in 1899 said:

> *A girl should learn to make a bed,*
> *To bake good biscuit, cake, and bread;*
> *To handle deftly brush and broom,*
> *And neatly tidy up a room.*

Grandmary allowed Samantha to help Mrs. Hawkins in the kitchen. Samantha learned to make dainty sandwiches for supper or tea. And she squeezed lemons on the juicer for lemon ice. But Samantha especially enjoyed baking apple brown Betty, jelly biscuits, and gingerbread!

When they made apple brown Betty, Samantha liked to put the apples onto the apple peeler and turn the crank. It was fun to see the peel come off in one long piece. Mrs. Hawkins thought the apple peeler was a silly invention. She said she could peel an apple just as well with a knife. But she had to admit that the machine peeled apples much faster than she could.

When they made jelly biscuits, Samantha loved using the sifter, rolling out the dough, and cutting the dough with round biscuit cutters. Sometimes when Mrs. Hawkins wasn't looking, Samantha sneaked a small piece of dough to eat!

Making gingerbread was quite an effort, but the smell of it baking in the oven for an afternoon tea treat made all the effort worthwhile. Samantha listened carefully to Mrs. Hawkins's advice on measuring ingredients and stirring them together. She was glad that Mrs. Hawkins liked her company. And Samantha was proud when Mrs. Hawkins told her she was becoming quite clever in the kitchen!

FAVORITE FOODS

Apple Brown Betty

•

Jelly Biscuits

•

Cream Cheese and Walnut Sandwiches

•

Chicken Salad Sandwiches

•

Gingerbread

•

Lemon Ice

Women cooking in their 1897 kitchen.

APPLE BROWN BETTY

Rich apple brown Betty melts in your mouth.

INGREDIENTS

Butter to grease
   baking pan
4 large apples
1½ cups bread crumbs
½ cup brown sugar
3 tablespoons butter
Cinnamon
⅓ cup milk
⅓ cup butter
⅓ cup powdered sugar
1 teaspoon vanilla

EQUIPMENT

9-inch-square baking pan
Vegetable peeler
Apple corer
Sharp knife
Cutting board
Measuring cups
   and spoons
Butter knife
Potholders
Small bowl
Spoon

DIRECTIONS   *6 servings*

Step 2

Step 3

Step 4

1. Preheat the oven to 375°. Spread butter over the bottom and sides of the pan.

2. Have an adult help you peel the skins off the apples.

3. Insert the apple corer into the center of each apple and twist it to cut around the core. Then remove the cores from the apples.

4. Have an adult help you slice the apples into ¼-inch rings on the cutting board.

5. Cover the bottom of the baking pan with ½ cup bread crumbs.

6. Arrange half of the apple slices on top of the crumbs.

7. Sprinkle ¼ cup brown sugar on the apples.

8. Use the butter knife to cut 1 tablespoon of the butter into small pieces and lay them on top of the brown sugar. Sprinkle cinnamon on top.

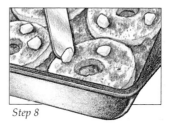
Step 8

9. Add a second layer of bread crumbs and repeat Steps 6 through 8.

10. Top the apple brown Betty with ½ cup bread crumbs and 1 tablespoon of butter cut into small pieces. Pour ⅓ cup milk evenly over the top.

11. Bake the apple brown Betty on the center rack of the oven for 1 hour.

KITCHEN GADGETS

Many newfangled kitchen gadgets, like the mechanical apple peeler, made cooking easier. With a turn of the crank and a roll of the gears, the apple was peeled.

12. While the apple brown Betty bakes, begin to make a "hard sauce." Cut ⅓ cup butter into small chunks. Put them into the bowl to soften.

13. Have an adult remove the apple brown Betty from the oven. Let it cool in the baking pan while you finish making the sauce.

14. Add the powdered sugar to the softened butter. Press the butter and sugar against the side of the bowl. Then stir them until they are smooth and creamy. Stir in the vanilla.

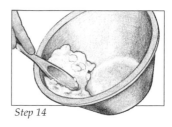
Step 14

15. Dot the top of the warm apple Betty with hard sauce so the sauce melts. ❧

JELLY BISCUITS

These biscuits are baked with jelly in the center.

INGREDIENTS

2 cups flour
4 teaspoons baking powder
2 tablespoons sugar
$1/2$ teaspoon salt
$1/2$ cup shortening
$3/4$ cup milk
Flour for cutting board
   and rolling pin
$1/2$ cup jelly or jam

EQUIPMENT

Sifter
Medium mixing bowl
Measuring cups
   and spoons
Pastry cutter *(optional)*
Fork
Cutting board
Rolling pin
2- to 3-inch round cookie
   cutter or drinking glass
Spatula
Cookie sheet
1-inch round cookie cutter
   or bottle cap
Potholders

DIRECTIONS   *18 biscuits*

1. Preheat the oven to 425°.

Steps 2, 3

2. Put the sifter into the mixing bowl. Measure the flour, baking powder, sugar, and salt into the sifter. Then sift them into the bowl.

3. Add the shortening. Use the pastry cutter or a fork to blend the shortening and flour mixture until it becomes a coarse meal.

4. Add in the milk and blend with the fork until the mixture forms a soft ball of dough.

5. Sprinkle a little flour on the cutting board. Spread it evenly with your hands.

34

6. Put the ball of dough on the cutting board and knead the dough 12 times. To knead the dough, press down on it with the palms of your hands. Then fold it in half. Press it and fold it again. Add a little more flour if the dough sticks.

Step 6

7. Put more flour on the cutting board and rolling pin. Roll out the dough from the center to the edges until it is about $\frac{1}{4}$ inch thick.

Step 7

8. With the large cookie cutter or the glass, cut circles close together out of the dough.

Step 8

9. Use the spatula to move half the circles to the cookie sheet. Place them 1 inch apart.

10. With the small cookie cutter or bottle cap, cut a hole in the center of the remaining circles. Lift these rings onto the top of the biscuit circles on the cookie sheet.

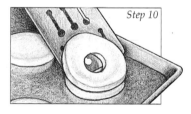
Step 10

11. Form a ball with the remaining dough, roll it out, and continue forming circles and rings until all the dough is used.

12. Put a teaspoon of jelly or jam into each ring.

13. Bake the jelly biscuits for 12 to 15 minutes, until they are golden brown. Have an adult remove the biscuits from the oven to cool.

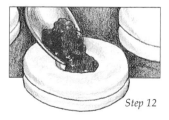
Step 12

CREAM CHEESE & WALNUT SANDWICHES

Cream cheese and walnut sandwiches are scrumptious for tea or for supper.

INGREDIENTS

8 ounces cream cheese
4 tablespoons butter
1/4 cup chopped walnuts
1/8 teaspoon nutmeg
1 tablespoon cream
1 teaspoon honey
12 pieces bread

EQUIPMENT

2 small mixing bowls
Measuring cups
  and spoons
Fork
Mixing spoon
Cutting board
Butter knife
Sharp knife

DIRECTIONS   *6 servings*

1. Soften the cream cheese in 1 mixing bowl by letting it sit at room temperature for 1 hour. In the other mixing bowl, soften the butter by letting it sit at room temperature for 1 hour.

2. Add the chopped walnuts, nutmeg, and cream to the cream cheese. Stir well with the fork.

3. Add the honey to the butter and mix well with the spoon.

4. Lay 6 slices of bread on the cutting board. Use the butter knife to spread the honey-butter on the bread. Then spread the cream cheese and nut filling on top.

5. Lay the remaining 6 slices of bread on top of the filling. Use the sharp knife to cut off the crusts. Then cut each sandwich into triangles, squares, or rectangles. 🐦

SUCCESSFUL SANDWICHES

A 1903 article offered this advice to sandwich makers: "Remember that bread must be cut thin, trimmed neatly, spread only lightly with butter, and cut into sandwiches of varying shapes; triangles always taste better than squares."

CHICKEN SALAD SANDWICHES

INGREDIENTS

2 cups cooked or canned
    chicken
2 celery ribs
2 hard-boiled eggs, peeled
2 tablespoons pickle relish
4 tablespoons mayonnaise
Salt and pepper
Softened butter
12 slices of bread

EQUIPMENT

Sharp knife
Cutting board
Measuring cups
    and spoons
Medium mixing bowl
Wooden spoon
Butter knife

Chicken salad was a favorite in Samantha's time, just as it is today.

DIRECTIONS   *6 servings*

1. Have an adult help you cut the chicken into very small cubes.

2. Have an adult help you cut off the ends of the celery ribs and chop the ribs into very small pieces.

3. Cut the hard-boiled eggs in very small pieces.

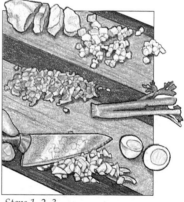

Steps 1, 2, 3

4. Put the chicken, celery, and eggs in the bowl. Add pickle relish, mayonnaise, and a sprinkle of salt and pepper. Mix well.

5. Spread butter on 6 slices of bread. Spread the chicken salad on the buttered slices.

6. Put the remaining 6 slices of bread on top.

7. Cut away the crusts. Then cut the sandwiches into triangles, squares, or rectangles. 🐚

HOW TO HARD-BOIL EGGS

Put the eggs into a pan and cover them with cold water. Heat the water until it bubbles rapidly. Then turn off the heat and cover the pan. After 15 minutes, have an adult run cold water over the eggs. Then peel them.

GINGERBREAD

Gingerbread is a tempting treat, served warm or cool.

INGREDIENTS

Butter to grease
  baking dish
$1/4$ cup butter
1 egg
$1/2$ cup buttermilk
$1/2$ cup light molasses
$1^1/2$ cups flour
$1/4$ cup sugar
1 teaspoon baking powder
$1/4$ teaspoon baking soda
$1/4$ teaspoon salt
$1/4$ teaspoon ground cloves
2 teaspoons ground ginger
1 teaspoon cinnamon
Powdered sugar *(optional)*
Whipped cream *(optional)*

EQUIPMENT

9-inch round baking dish
Measuring cups
  and spoons
Small saucepan
Medium mixing bowl
Wire whisk
Large mixing bowl
Fork
Mixing spoon
Toothpick
Potholders

DIRECTIONS   *6 servings*

1. Preheat the oven to 350°. Grease the baking dish with butter.

2. Melt $1/4$ cup butter in the saucepan over low heat. Be careful not to let the butter burn. Then turn off the heat and let the butter cool.

3. Crack the egg into the medium mixing bowl. Beat the egg with the wire whisk.

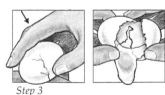

Step 3

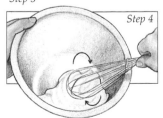

Step 4

4. Add the buttermilk, molasses, and melted butter to the egg. Mix well.

5. Measure the flour, sugar, baking powder, baking soda, salt, cloves, ginger, and cinnamon into the large mixing bowl. Mix them together using the fork.

6. Pour the liquid ingredients into the flour mixture. Stir to make a smooth batter.

7. Pour the batter into the baking dish.

8. Bake the gingerbread on the center rack of the oven for 25 to 30 minutes.

9. Check to see if the gingerbread is done by inserting a toothpick into the center. If the toothpick comes out clean, the gingerbread is done.

10. Have an adult take the gingerbread out of the oven. Let it sit for about 5 minutes to serve it warm. Or let the gingerbread cool to room temperature.

11. Cut the gingerbread. Serve it with powdered sugar or whipped cream on top. 🐌

GINGER

Ginger is a spice that originally came from China and India. Some people used ginger as a medicine to cure stomachaches and colds.

From the book *Samantha's Surprise*

GINGERBREAD HOUSES

At Christmastime, children like Samantha loved to help build houses out of hard gingerbread. They used gumdrops, sugar wafers, caramel squares, and honey sticks for decorations.

LEMON ICE

Cool lemon ice makes a perfect refreshment on a warm day!

INGREDIENTS

4 lemons
1 orange
4 cups water
1½ cups sugar

EQUIPMENT

Sharp knife
Cutting board
Juicer
Bowl to fit juicer
Measuring cups
2-quart saucepan
Wooden spoon
Large mixing bowl
Strainer
Plastic container with lid
Large metal spoon

DIRECTIONS   *1 quart*

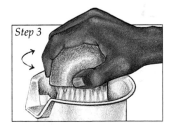

1. Have an adult help you cut the lemons and orange in half on the cutting board.

2. Set the juicer over the bowl so the edges fit tightly.

3. Squeeze the juice out of the lemon and orange halves by turning them back and forth on the juicer while pushing down.

4. Measure the water and sugar into the saucepan. Stir them well.

5. Heat the mixture over medium heat until it *boils*, or bubbles rapidly, for 10 minutes.

6. Have an adult help you pour the water and sugar mixture into the large mixing bowl.

ICE DELIVERY

Blocks of ice were delivered in horse-drawn wagons. Deliverymen used large tongs to pick up the ice and lift it onto their shoulders. Then they carried the ice into kitchens like Sumuntha's and put it into iceboxes. On hot summer days, the iceman would give children chips of ice as cool treats!

7. Pour the juice through the strainer into the mixing bowl. Stir the mixture well. Then let it cool.

8. Pour the mixture into the plastic container and cover it. Freeze the lemon ice for several hours until it is hard.

9. Use the large spoon to scrape shavings off the top of the lemon ice and shape them into scoop-size servings. 🍋

HARVESTING ICE

*This picture shows men cutting huge pieces of ice from a lake. The ice will be hauled away by horses to a building called an **icehouse**. The ice had to last until the next winter's ice harvest!*

PLAN A TEA PARTY

ETIQUETTE

Girls practiced proper behavior, or **etiquette,** *at tea parties. They never put their elbows on the table, and they sat up straight instead of slouching. When food was passed, it was proper to say "thank you," not "thanks," which was considered lazy and disrespectful.*

In Samantha's time, women loved to gather with their families and friends for a half hour or so in the late afternoon to talk, drink tea, and have some dainty sweets. Young girls copied their mothers by having their own friends over for tea parties. You can plan a tea party of your own that's just like a party Samantha might have had.

Start by making proper invitations. If you can, deliver the invitations in person. Decorate small pieces of notepaper, and then write an invitation such as this one:

> *Miss _____ requests the pleasure of Miss _____'s company on Tuesday evening, June 13th, from four to six o'clock at a tea party.* *R.S.V.P.* *

*"RSVP" is short for the French phrase *Répondez s'il vous plaît* (ray-pon-DAY see voo play). It means "please reply."

❧ AN AFTERNOON TEA PARTY

Set up small tables, each seating four to six people, in the living room or dining room, or on the porch. When the guests are seated, offer each one a choice of tea or cocoa. Fill each guest's cup and pass it to her. Be sure to pass cream or milk, lemon slices, and sugar, too. Simple food, such as bread with butter and jam, can look pretty if the bread is sliced very thin and trimmed of crusts. You might also want to offer plates of dainty cookies, small iced cakes called *petit fours*, bonbons, or nuts.

❧ A Color Tea

Color teas were popular in the early 1900s. The hostess chose a color and then planned to have everything on the table in that color—including the dishes, napkins, decorations, and even the food! If you have a color tea, ask your parents if they have a solid-colored tablecloth (a bedsheet will do), and then find dishes or paper plates and napkins to match. Try to think of a centerpiece and delicious treats of the same color! It might be fun to ask your guests to wear clothes of the chosen color, too.

❧ A Garden Tea Party

In warm weather, girls like Samantha sometimes had tea parties in their gardens. Invite your guests to a garden party, and set up the tea tables on the lawn. Play an outdoor game, such as croquet, before the tea party. You can also play "fish pond." To play, put a tub in the garden. Then put many small, inexpensive gifts into the tub. The gifts should be individually wrapped, and each one should be tied with a large loop. Give each guest the same number of tries to capture a gift using a fishing rod with a large hook on the end of the line.

❧ A Doll Tea Party

Children like Samantha loved to invite their friends over for a doll tea party. Even Grandmary had tea parties with her dolls when she was a girl! When you make your invitations, ask each guest to bring her favorite doll in its finest clothes. Have tiny cakes and cookies to serve the dolls (and yourselves!). Use a miniature tea set if you have one, or the smallest cups and dishes you can find in your home.

FINGER BOWLS

In Samantha's time, a small bowl half full of warm water was placed on a dessert plate near each place setting. Often a thin lemon slice or flower petals floated on top. After eating, guests dipped their fingers into the water and then dried them on their napkins.

PLACE CARDS

Proper seating was important at turn-of-the-century tables. Small place cards showed guests where to sit. The most important female guest was seated to the right of the host. The most important male guest was seated to the left of the hostess.

Food

You can prepare and serve chicken salad sandwiches or cream cheese and walnut sandwiches, gingerbread, lemon ice, or jelly biscuits from this cookbook for your tea party. Send each guest home with a small box of extra treats to remember the party.

Place Settings

Use china if you can, or pretty paper plates. Alongside each plate, lay whatever knives, forks, or spoons you'll need for the party food and a large, neatly ironed and folded cloth napkin. Make a pretty place card for each guest.

Decorations

Unless you are planning to have a color tea, use a white tablecloth, which was standard in the early 1900s. Put a vase of flowers or a candle in a pretty candlestick in the center of the tea table.

Clothes

Large hair ribbons were popular in Samantha's time. You can make them out of wide ribbon or crepe paper for you and your guests to wear. Light-colored party clothes and *parasols*, or umbrellas used in the sun, were proper for garden parties.

Music

You might want to listen to popular Victorian songs like "Bicycle Built for Two" or "Sweet Adeline" during your tea party. Your local library may have a recording of songs like these played on a player piano or sung by a barbershop quartet—both were very popular in Samantha's day.

AMERICAN GIRLS PASTIMES™
Activities from the Past for Girls of Today

You'll enjoy all the Pastimes books about your favorite characters in The American Girls Collection®.

Learn to cook foods that Felicity, Kirsten, Addy, Samantha, and Molly loved with the Pastimes **COOKBOOKS**. They're filled with great recipes and fun party ideas.

Make the same crafts that your favorite American Girls character made. Each of the **CRAFT BOOKS** has simple step-by-step instructions and fascinating historical facts.

Imagine that you are your favorite American Girls character as you stage a play about her. Each of the **THEATER KITS** has four Play Scripts and a Director's Guide.

Learn about fashions of the past as you cut out the ten outfits in each of the **PAPER DOLL KITS**. Each kit also contains a make-it-yourself book plus historical fun facts.

There are **CRAFT KITS** for each character with directions and supplies to make 3 crafts from the Pastimes Craft Books. Craft Kits are available only through Pleasant Company's catalogue, which you can request by filling out the postcard below.

Turn the page to learn more about the other delights in The American Girls Collection. ⟶

I'm an American girl who loves to get mail. Please send me a catalogue of The American Girls Collection®:

My name is _____

My address is _____

City _____ State _____ Zip _____

Parent's signature_____

1961

And send a catalogue to my friend:

My friend's name is_____

Address _____

City_____ State _____ Zip _____

1225

THE AMERICAN GIRLS COLLECTION®

The American Girls Collection tells the stories of five lively nine-year-old girls who lived long ago—Felicity, Kirsten, Addy, Samantha, and Molly. You can read about their adventures in a series of beautifully illustrated books of historical fiction. By reading these books, you'll learn what growing up was like in times past.

There is also a lovable doll for each character with beautiful clothes and lots of wonderful accessories. The dolls and their accessories make the stories of the past come alive today for American girls like you.

The American Girls Collection is for you if you love to curl up with a good book. It's for you if you like to play with dolls and act out stories. It's for you if you want something so special that you will treasure it for years to come.

To learn more about The American Girls Collection, fill out the postcard on the other side of the page and mail it to Pleasant Company, or call **1-800-845-0005.** We will send you a free catalogue about all the books, dolls, dresses, and other delights in The American Girls Collection.